My Truths,

My Triumphs,

My God

By LaVerne Blackwell

First Edition

Biographical Publishing Company
Prospect, Connecticut

My Truths, My Triumphs, My God

First Edition

Published by:

Biographical Publishing Company
95 Sycamore Drive
Prospect, CT 06712-1493
Phone: 203-758-3661   Fax: 253-793-2618
e-mail: biopub@aol.com

Publisher's Cataloging-in-Publication Data
Blackwell, LaVerne
My Truths, My Triumphs, My God / by LaVerne Blackwell.
1st ed.
p. cm.
ISBN (alk. Paper): 1-7338120-6-7
13-Digit ISBN: 9781733812061
1. Title. 2. African American autobiography. 3. Family history.
Dewey Decimal Classification: 920 Biography
BISAC Subjects:
    BIO002010   Biography & Autobiography /Cultural, Ethnic
                        & Regional / African American & Black
    BIO000000   Biography & Autobiography / General
    BIO018000   Biography & Autobiography / Religious
Library of Congress Control Number: 2020915429

Acknowledgment

My first thanks and praise belongs to my God who has sustained and provided for me all of my years.

I thank my loving husband, Calvin Blackwell, Sr., for all of his help and encouragement while writing this book. He continued to print and read each page and for giving his advice.

I thank our daughter, Shanyelle Young, for planting the idea in my head, to keep me busy during the pandemic.

I thank my cousin, Yolanda Archer-Lee, for helping me come up with the title for my book.

My thanks also to my lifelong friend, Evangelist Barbara M. Fountain, for her prayers and our touching and agreeing almost weekly about my book.

My family, I love you all so much for your love and support throughout my life, helping me to become the woman I am today.

By you I have been upheld from my birth.

Psalms 71: 6

If two of you agree on earth
concerning anything that they ask,
it will be done for them by My Father in heaven.

Matthew 18:19

PART ONE

I was born on February 21, 1949 in St. Phillips Hospital, in Richmond, Virginia. My grandmother named me Ida LaVerne Archer. I was brought from the hospital to my grandmother Sallie B. Archer's home, which was at 607 N. Henry Street, Richmond, Virginia.

LaVerne with
grandmother,
Sallie Baker-Archer

I do not remember anything about my life until about age two and knowing that my grandmother became my "first love." I remember her taking such good care of me, washing and dressing me, making my breakfast, eggs and fried salt pork. We went out often, mostly to Broad Street, but often to a bootleg house where she would buy her drinks. She always wore a hat and put a bow in my hair. She wold not allow me to play with the children if they were not clean; she would keep me sitting on her lap. Upon returning home, there was often yelling from my mother, telling her to stop taking LaVerne to those "bootleg houses." As time moved on, I began to realize that my grandmother was an alcoholic. However, she took very good care of me and I felt safe in her care. I loved being with my grandmother; she told me daily how much she loved me and I told her that I loved her just as often.

My sister, Francine Archer, was born about two years after me. I do not remember very much about Francine. I had three uncles who also lived with us: my uncle Zick, who was named after his father, Williams Sears Archer, uncle Frank, Irving Franklin Archer and uncle Bubba, Joseph Rudolph Archer. My mother, Mary Louise Archer, worked as a live-in or was out often. I can remember uncle Zick combing and braiding my hair sometimes. I really do not remember much of my mother during that time.

I remember at one time my grandmother not being there for what seemed to me a very long time. Even today, as I write this, I can remember the tremendous sadness that I felt. I asked everyone, "Where is my grandmother?" They told me that she was in the hospital and would be there for a long time. I know that I was sad and felt like I shut down for that period of time. My grandmother finally came home from the hospital and I was so happy to see her. I know I cried. However, there was something so different about her; she was quite and sad and didn't take me anywhere. She spent her days just sitting in her chair. I would rub her swollen feet. I asked uncle Zick what was wrong with my grandmother and he explained to me that while at the hospital, they did something to her brain to help her stop drinking alcohol. It was at this time that I met my oldest uncle when he brought his family to Richmond, from Amelia, Virginia to see grandmother. Uncle James Archer came to visit with his son, Boo, also James Archer. I can tell you today that I fell in love with my only male cousin that day. He was so kind and so much fun, but what I remember the most was how he took care of us, not letting anything happen to us. Today, my cousin Boo is the same way. I love him just as much as I loved him back then. Whenever I visit him, he is still the same; he still wants to take care of me. Uncle James' wife was aunt Vick; they later had a daughter, Sylvia, who was a year younger that I. Much later, they had a baby girl, Joan.

George and Mary
Archer-Bunn

In October, 1953 I remember my mother standing in my grandmother's living room getting married to George Albert Bunn, who adopted Francine and me. I became Ida LaVerne Bunn and Francine became Francine Bunn, and George A. Bunn became Daddy to us. We spent time going to

Amelia visiting with his stepfather, Mr. Blaine and some of his other family members. We visited Uncle James and his family during that time also.

Daddy was around for a short period of time and he left to go overseas as he was in the U.S. Army. He was stationed at the army base in Chinon, France.

I remember the army car coming to take us to the base in Richmond for immunization shots, preparing us to relocate to France. I hated to get in the car because I would get car sick every time. They started bringing oranges for me to eat and I began to look forward to the military car coming, but could not stand the immunizations. It was always a fight to catch me and hold me down. Francine was tougher than I was. The day finally arrived for us to leave Richmond and take a train to New York to board the ship, Rose, for our journey to France. I was angry and sad; I did not want to leave my first love, my grandmother Sallie. She told me to be a big girl and I would be back one day. We sailed on the Rose for 13 days and nights and I was seasick for most of those days. We shared a three-bed cabin on the ship. I had to grow up on that ship, my mother went out most evenings after putting us to bed and telling me to take care of Francine but be sure not to tell daddy that she went out at night.

Upon our arrival in France, after those long thirteen days, Daddy was there to pick us up and we moved into our new home in Chinon. Shortly after arriving in Chinon, Daddy became my second love. He spent so much time with me, teaching me so many things about God, prayer and how to be smart. He taught me to speak French quickly as he realized that I would have to translate for my mother when he was not around. I picked up the language very quickly. One of Daddy's jobs was to drive the military school bus, picking up the children to attend school on the base. Once I started school, he would pick me up and I would ride the bus along with the other children

Francine was a beautiful child and stayed home with my mother before she started school. My mother was very social and met many of the army wives who often wanted to take Francine out because she was so pretty. It seemed that no one took me out as I was definitely not as pretty or as social as Francine or my mother. However, there was a military couple that lived across the street, Mr. Jimmy and Mrs. Carol, who took a liking to me. When Mr. Jimmy worked at night, Mrs. Carol would let me spend the night with her. My mother told me that I could not go with Francine overnight because I wet the bed, but I never wet Mrs. Carol's bed and always enjoyed spending time with her.

PART TWO

Our lives changed once we moved to France. We ate healthy meals daily; my mother cooked a three-course breakfast and a three-course dinner daily. I really could see a change in our lives. I asked Daddy why did we ate such a big breakfast every morning. He answered that it is how he is custom to eating. Well that is not how we were custom to eating in Richmond, but were able to eat good on the ship. We had a very nice home and plenty of nice clothes. My little mind began to think we were rich and I began to enjoy life. Daddy and I attended church services on the military base. I remember enjoying the services and hymns. I don't remember ever attending a church prior to that time.

I was enrolled in school on the military base. I loved school and had several friends from different countries and different backgrounds. I was the only African American girl in my class, and there was one African American male in my class. Everyone else was bi-racial, many were from Germany. We spoke English in school but learned the French language. I loved speaking French and was proud that I spoke the language so well. My neighborhood friends were French so I wanted to be able to play with them after school and on weekends.

Daddy signed me up for the Brownies Troop and I was so proud to move on up to Girl Scouts in a nice ceremony. I was always proud to wear my uniform; it made me feel important. Daddy explained to me the importance of this commitment and honor.

We soon had a nanny that lived with us; her name was Lucy. I don't remember very much about Lucy other than she was to help care for us and help my mother around the house.

My mother was often out with her new friends and again, Francine was so pretty that everyone wanted to take her places. I remember my mother often saying to watch out for Francine as she was so pretty, we were afraid that the Gypsies would steal her. I spent lots of time with Daddy so I was not too bothered with feeling any kind of way about Francine being so pretty and spoiled by everyone. Daddy took me to the jewelry store and got my ears pierced. I cried because it hurt so bad, but after a few days, I thought I looked pretty.

Daddy had one friend named Shorty. Shorty visited often and stayed for dinner sometimes. We were very comfortable with him. I think I was about seven years old when we came home from school and no adult was home. Shorty came by to visit. He gave us some money and gave Francine some extra money and told her to go the store to buy some candy for the two of us. While she was gone, Shorty sexually abused me and left soon after. I did not tell my mother or my sister, but when Daddy came home, I told him exactly what happened. He asked me several question about what happened, and I was very specific; he did not penetrate me but still abused me. Daddy left the house and from that day til this, we never saw Shorty again. It was because of this that Lucy moved in full time. We never had a problem after that; someone was home with us at all times.

Father, George A. Bunn

We lived in a neighborhood where there was a butcher shop, a bakery and a café was next door. Our house was next to a long alleyway where Francine and I played often. My father spanked me one time in my life and that was because it was raining and the water always ran down that alleyway. I decided to take Francine's new shoes and put them in the water and laughed as they rolled down the alley in that water. My mother was so angry and when Daddy came home, I could not stop laughing at what I did. Daddy put my head between his legs and tore my butt up. He never had a problem out of me since. I learned my lesson after that one spanking.

Life for us started changing somewhat. Lucy moved out into her own apartment. However, Daddy took me to visit her a couple of times. One night he did not show up for dinner and my mother demanded that I take her to Lucy's apartment. We walked in the rain, across the bridge to Lucy's house. Upon arriving on her street, we saw Daddy's car parked outside. My mother and I looked in the window and saw Daddy's uniform shirt on the chair, GA Bunn. My mother banged on that door until Lucy answered and the fight began. I stood there yelling for them to stop. Daddy never came downstairs, but Lucy's sister came down and threw water on my mother. We left and walked back across that bridge with my mother yelling the entire time. I really don't know what happened when he came home. A few months later, Daddy took me to visit Lucy and my baby sister, Jackie. I believe that he also took Francine and me there another time. We never saw Lucy or Jackie after that time. As far as I know, Jackie was Daddy's only biological child.

We moved to another apartment a few months later and our new nanny was Nicole. We loved Nicole, she was young, pretty and lots of fun. Francine and I loved spending time with her. One Sunday morning, Daddy was sitting at the table finishing his breakfast and my mother began to yell at him and came into out bedroom where we were watching Nicole put make up on. My mother grabbed Nicole and began to fight her, yelling that she better leave her husband alone. Daddy had admitted that he and Nicole we having an affair. Nicole moved that day and Francine and I talked about how angry we were.

Other than those affairs, we had a good life. We had everything children could want or need. My mother lived a good life. She had many friends and spent time shopping, getting her hair done and generally enjoying her good life.

In June, 1959, we boarded another ship, Queen Elizabeth, to head back to the United States. I was sea sick the first few days, but Daddy took care of me and I felt better. This trip was twelve days long; it seemed so much longer because I was so excited to be returning to Richmond to see my grandmother. I tell you that I could not wait and kept asking how much longer. We had to stay in New York for two weeks, Daddy took us to Central Park often to play. I only wanted to get to Richmond. However, Daddy told us that we would fly into Philadelphia and visit with his sister, Aunt Shirley, for a few days. I liked Aunt Shirley the minute I met her. I liked her so much that I wanted to change my name to Shirley LaVerne, dropping Ida. We had a great time visiting with Aunt Shirley and her husband, (I cannot remember his name). Although it was a great time, I was anxious to see my grandmother.

I had no idea that returning to Richmond, our lives would change forever.

PART THREE

We finally flew in to Richmond, and took a Taxi to my grandmother's house. I can tell you that I the first person out of that taxi, seeing my grandmother standing in her yard waiting for us. I almost knocked her over when I jumped in her arms. I could not take my eyes off her beautiful face. She was crying and I was crying. I know she greeted everyone else but she took me in the house, holding my hand and saying I have a surprise for you. She took me straight to her television set. I asked what was that because I had never seen a TV before. She turned it on and the Three Stooges were on. I stared at it and laughed as we watched. In France our entertainment was listening to Elvis Presley, LaVerne Baker and Rick Nelson. I could dance to Elvis' *Blue Suede Shoes*.

Uncle Frank and Uncle Joe (Bubba), the men in my life

Uncle Frank and Uncle Bubba came over after we got there. They hugged us all but immediately asked if they could take us to the movies. Daddy said yes, and they both wanted to take

Francine. Neither wanted to take me, so Daddy finally told them that I should stay home, because I forgot to brush my teeth that morning. Truthfully, I did not care because I wanted to stay home with my grandmother. We learned that my uncles did not live there anymore. they had been placed in foster care. My grandmother had become a true alcoholic while we were away. We stayed with my grandmother for a short period. I don't remember Daddy staying with us.

Aunt Lila Archer

Daddy came to move us to Decatur Street on the south side of Richmond. I think he had been working on that for a while because it was done so quickly. We moved into a very large house with a big front porch. We lived on the third floor, with two bedrooms, a kitchen and dining room. Daddy left and returned to the Army. We did not see him anymore for over one year. We became close to the families that lived on the first and second floors. It was there that I met my soon to be Aunt Lila. Her mother, stepfather and siblings lived on the second floor and Lila lived near with her granny.

Her cousin and her children lived on the first floor. My

mother started a job as a domestic worker and Lila's mother kept an eye out for Francine and me. The summer ended and we started school. Uncle Frank and Uncle Bubba enlisted in the Army Reserve. I did not see my grandmother often after that.

I entered 5th grade at Blackwell Jr. High School. I was scared out of my mind. First of all my teachers were all African Americans, as were all of the students. I felt like an outcast. I had never attended a school of all African Americans. The teachers would always ask me to speak French or just to talk, because I had an accent. I was very shy in this new environment. I was placed in the class with all of the smart and wealthier children and I was poor as the church mouse. One of the teachers asked if I would like to become a safety patrol and I said yes. Lila attended that school also. She was in the eighth grade and I looked up to her because she was popular and I often told her how uncomfortable I felt. She encouraged me to try to meet some of the children in my grade. She would come visit her mother everyday. It was here at Blackwell Jr. High where I met my best friend, Barbara Mashore. We are still best friends today.

Living on Decatur Street was life changing for me. We did not have decent clothing, no money and I was always hungry. My mother worked and had very little money. I often complained because of our circumstances and was told to be quiet. I would come home from school and open the refrigerator to a half can of Pet Milk. This is when my mother really depended on me and I had to grow up and become the little adult. My mother would have me go with her to fill out applications to purchase furniture. I would go with her to our landlord to speak to him on her behalf or go to him to borrow money for food or oil to heat the apartment. My mother was deaf in one ear and I knew this but I was resentful that I had to do all of the adult work, including taking care of my sister everyday. I was angry most of the time now. I hated living like this. We had mice all over the place. I am still petrified of mice today.

That following June, I was suppose to spend the week with my grandmother. That Friday evening a woman pulled up to our house looking for my mother. I asked her who should I say is looking for her. I thought it was one of the rich ladies that she worked for. The woman told me that she was my mother's Aunt Ida, my grand-mother's sister. (I was later told that is the aunt who my grandmother named me after.) I ran upstairs to tell my mother that her aunt was outside. Maybe she was coming to take me to my grandmother's house. But I soon found out that she came to tell us that Grandmother had died. I cannot tell you how broken my heart was. I could not cry at her funeral. My grief was inside of my soul, where it remains today.

Uncle Frank met Lila and they got married and had their first daughter, Joan Louise. Joan was named after my mother, Mary Louise. We all lived together for a while and Lila took care of Francine and me. She did most of the cooking and cleaning. She kept my hair looking nice to help me feel better about myself. She taught me how to care for myself as a female.

Uncle Frank moved his family across town and we moved to 16th Street, which was a very nice two bedroom apartment. Again, I had to take care of my sister and myself, and have dinner ready when my mother came home. My anger was starting to progress. One of the teachers asked me to help her out on Saturdays and I was happy to make a little money. I went to her house for a few hours on Saturdays and she gave me a couple of dollars. I did not do any work, just talked to her and her son. I saw how other lived and swore at that young age that I would live a decent life when I grew up.

We moved again, three times in one and a half years. Daddy came to see us out of the blue. I was now angry with him for leaving us and allowing us to live so poorly. He asked us to move to Alexandria, Virginia with him, telling us that we would have our own rooms, and new clothes, and would live in a big house and attend a good school. Although I was so angry, I did not want to leave my mother because there was no one else to take care of her. I knew I would have a better life living with Daddy. I told him that I would think about it. He said he would come to get us for a week's visit on Father's Day. Father's Day came and Daddy did not come during the day, so my mother, my sister and her boyfriend went to visit some friends. I went to a dance with my friends. I was disappointed because I had told my friends that I would be going to stay with my father for a week.

However, when the dance was over, walking home, I saw Daddy's car and got so excited. I told my friends, "See he's here and I am leaving."

I walked in the house and asked Daddy why was he so late getting here. I don't remember what he said but I started packing for Francine and myself. Daddy was acting a little strange. I knew he did not ever drink alcohol, and could not understand his behavior. He began to ask me about boyfriends. I told him that I did not have any boyfriends. He said he wanted to teach me about boys, and started to become inappropriate. I walked in to the living room and told him to wait, I would be right back. He forgot that he had taught me to always be smart and think ahead. I opened the living room window and ran so hard and fast to where my mother was and ran up the steps, hit the door hard one time and passed out. I woke up crying and told them what had almost happened. The took me to the police station and after a lot of questioning, they called the MPs (Military Police). We met back at our house and Daddy was laying in the same spot I had left him in, still with his shoes and shirt off. The MPs put him in handcuffs and put him in the paddy wagon. He looked at me and said look what you did to me on Father's Day. This is a memory I will have in my head for the rest of my life. I was too young to think this behavior was out of character for him and he would never do anything to hurt me. I knew he loved me and I loved him very much.

My uncles came over the next day yelling that they

should take us away from my mother because she could not parent us correctly. She could not keep us safe. At that point of my 12-year-old life, I was more confused than ever and my thoughts were, "Am I going to make it?"

We went to court three times. Each time, Daddy had more lawyers, and my mother yelled at me each time saying that she did not believe me and had to take off work for this. The third time in court, I stood up and said it did not happen. I was so afraid of all of his lawyers and angry because my mother did not believe me. I felt so alone. No one cared about LaVerne and no one was there to support me. I now understand that my mother did not know how to support me.

A couple of weeks after the court issue that August, we move again, this time, across town, to a new school and new friends. The third week of August, my mother told us that she was moving to Atlantic City with her boyfriend to get a better job and make more money. Francine and I would stay with Uncle Frank and Aunt Lila for a short period. She said she would send us money and come to get us soon. I yelled that they had three kids and lived in the projects and could not keep us. But she had spoken to them and worked it out. Needless to say, she did not send money, nor come to get us. I would call her and Uncle Frank and Aunt Lila would call her. She promised that she was coming back to get us, but did not have any money to send us. Uncle Frank and Aunt Lila gave us whatever we needed and provided a stable home. But I knew this was a temporary situation.

Christmas was coming and they dis not have money to buy us gifts, so they called Daddy and he came to Richmond with money and gifts I did not want to see him so I stayed upstairs He asked me to come say hello to him. I slowly made my way downstairs, feeling safe because I knew that Uncle Frank and Aunt Lila would protect me. When I came downstairs, I saw all of the beautiful gifts he had purchased for Francine and I only had two games.

Two months later, in early February, Uncle Frank and Aunt Lila told us that they had spoken to Daddy and they were taking us to live with him because they were going to be evicted because we had been there since August. They were only suppose to keep us for two weeks. I can tell you that I had a break down fit. I actually screamed the entire drive, and they cried the entire time. I used curse words that I had never heard. It was ugly. I was afraid to have to live with Daddy after what I had encountered on Father's Day. I really wanted to run away but had nowhere to run to. I now felt there was no one to help LaVerne.

Arriving at Daddy's large and beautiful home, we found him in his pajamas; he was sick but I did not know what was wrong with him. We met his girlfriend and I immediately knew that this was not going to be a pleasant stay. Uncle Frank and Aunt Lila had a serious conversation with Daddy and his girlfriend, with instructions that no one at all should put their hands on me.

They left and I cried harder, thinking that this nightmare would end soon. However, it did not and we were shown to our beautiful rooms. His girlfriend was a nurse who worked nights. They had a woman who was there to help care for us. The girlfriend purchased many nice clothes for Francine and she bought me two matching outfits, one blue and one green, with matching socks. Daddy spent most days in his room; we rarely saw him. She registered us for school but I never attended for some reason, maybe paperwork, etc. Late that following Thursday night, I heard a loud thump coming from his room. I got out of bed and found Daddy on the floor. I don't remember who I called but the ambulance came and took him to the hospital, where he stayed until he passed the following month. He had a tumor on his brain.

His girlfriend did not like me at all and showed me in many ways that she did not like me and I did not like her at all. That Saturday morning, the woman who helped care for us, was making breakfast and called us down to eat. The girlfriend told her not to feed me because I was so bad and disrespectful. Already angry at everyone, I jumped the entire flight of stairs onto her and would not stop hitting her. The woman pulled me off of her. I called my aunt and uncle and they drove to Alexandria immediately. With my uncle along with them, my aunt yelled so much and threatened the girlfriend with bodily harm if she ever touched me again. Uncle Bubba threatened to shoot her. We all called my mother to let her know what happened and she needed to come get us immediately. My mother came that Monday. We went to see Daddy and the doctor told us that he was very sick with a tumor on his brain. He was hospitalized in Walter Reed Veterans Hospital, where he passed away. An Army social worker met with us and directed us where to go to obtain benefits. We stayed until the paperwork was completed and left with all of the necessary telephone numbers.

PART FOUR

My mother took us back to Atlantic City with her. I was 13 years old. We moved in with her and her boyfriend on Drexel Avenue. My mother, Francine and I slept together in one bed. Her boyfriend did not stay with us. We got the call on March 10th that Daddy had passed away that morning. We never got a chance to say good-by or attend his funeral. We were told that the monthly benefits should start soon and, as well, death benefits.

My mother took us to register for school. I was suppose to go to the 7th grade as I had attended 7th grade before leaving Richmond. The Board of Education gave me an aptitude test and I went to the 9th grade at Atlantic City High School. I was proud to jump so far ahead in school but was afraid to go to high school. I got in trouble the first week because I was told by my new friends to call this woman and threaten her, which I did but gave her my name as Ida LaVerne Bunn. The juvenile detective came to school the next day and I told him that I was just doing what my new friend told me to do. Needless to say that was end of my friendship with her. The following week I met a new friend from North Carolina who had just moved across the street. We looked alike and became fast friends until her death at a young age.

One month later we moved around the corner to Adriatic Avenue, a nice place with two bedrooms. My mother's boyfriend moved in with us and tried to be a father figure to us. But by this time, Francine and I were not having it. I met more friends and started to become a problem in school and at home. I met another friend who exhibited behavior problems like me. We became fast friends and remain friends today. She had just returned from Virginia, as she was having issues the previous year, and was sent to Virginia. We had lots of fun and hung out after school daily. We called ourselves a little clique and we agreed that we would get all of our friends from uptown on the last day of school and fight another group of girls. I did not fight but was in the crowd and started having a bad reputation as a fighter. They did fight and I was there and was arrested along with everyone else that day. The juvenile detective told me that he knew where I was headed because I was with the wrong crowd. I begged him not to put me in a cell and promised I would do better He put us in the cell for an overnight stay. I tell you I cried the entire night.

The next day, my mother was there along with the other parents, and she hit me several times in front of everyone. She told me that my clothes were packed. After a bath she was putting me on bus to Richmond. I was so ashamed to face my aunt and uncle after spending the night in jail. However, I stayed in Richmond until it was time to start my sophomore year. My mother and sister had moved to Grammercy Place upon my return.

The apartment was a one bedroom with a bed that often broke down when we sat on it.

At this time, I really start to play hooky from school. I pretended to be my mother saying something crazy like, "I would be out for one week because I had the measles." They requested a note upon my return, and I forged that too. One time I had to call Uncle Bubba and beg him to call the school for me. We played hooky at each other's homes. But one day we all came to my house thinking my mother had left for work, but when I put the key in the lock, my mother opened the door. Someone had told her that I was bringing several kids home as soon as she left for work. We ran from her and she met us at each corner. We laughed for a long time after that, but we never went back to my house after that. All of my friends were afraid of my mother because she yelled all of the time.

We moved to Congress Avenue that summer and I asked my mother if my friend Barbara Mashore could come up from Richmond so we could get jobs. She said yes and Barbara came up every summer to work until her senior year in high school. I truly started working at age 14 by telling the motel owner that I was 16 years old. We were always paid in cash. At the end of the summers, Barbara and I would take a bus to Philadelphia to shop for school clothes. We had so much in common and basically enjoyed each other's friendship and really never had any disagreements. Our friendship remains the same today.

That next school year found me so out of order that I knew I was headed for real trouble. Our benefits started coming in about that time and I thought we were rich. We had out own bedrooms and I had a telephone in my room. My mother bought us a large console TV. We had one problem at that time which caused us stress. My mother started seeing this guy who had one finger missing. She started spending our money on him. He became abusive towards her and sexually inappropriate with Francine and me. But my mother never believed us, saying we just did not want her to be happy.

That summer Barbara came up as usual and he was inappropriate with both of us by sneaking in my bedroom early that morning. We jumped up and ran downstairs and sat on the couch to discuss what had just happened to us. My mother woke early as she normally did and asked us why we were up so early. We told her what had happened to us and she started yelling about us telling lies on her boyfriend and Barbara should go home and not come back. I stood up to her and told her that he was a loser and took her upstairs and showed her where he had masturbated on my sister's bed. She still did not believe us and swore that we just did not want her to be happy.

That school year I began to fight and disobey everything that my mother told me to do. I was wild and knew it. It was like a person took control over my entire head. My letter writings to God was almost daily. I was forever asking for forgiveness of my sins and behaviors.

I would punch someone that looked at me wrong. My mother sent us to church but did not go herself. I got baptized the year before and celebrated with my friends; no adult showed up. I hated myself and I hated life. The boyfriend continued to live there. My sister ran away with one of her friends. She was picked up by the police after two weeks. My mother sent me to see what was going on and Francine said she rather stay in jail instead of coming back home. I was upset but could not change our lives. We were both out of control. But if a fight went down, we both went down with the fight.

Ida Bunn, just before being expelled from high school

The high school told me that I would be expelled as soon as I became of legal age, 16. I laughed and told them they would never expel me. However, on my 16th birthday, I was called into the office with my mother and was officially expelled. I was in shock and did not have a plan in place because I never thought it would happen. Many of my friends had dropped out to have children or get married. I believe I was the last one of my friends to be in school. Now I am out. God what now?

PART FIVE

At the age of 16 years old, I was expelled from Atlantic City High School due to my out of control, juvenile delinquent behaviors. I decided that I should try a new life, in my safety net. I called Uncle Frank and Aunt Lila to explain my situation and ask if I could move there with them until I secured employment and an apartment. They had a long discussion about my poor choices but I could come there and try to start over. They let me know how disappointed they were. They thought I would be the first family member to attend college. I told them that was my plan but things did not turn out that way. Uncle Bubba was very disappointed and actually called my mother again to tell her off.

I took a bus to Richmond a couple days later, and I was happy to be there. I called my friend, Barbara and she

LaVerne and best friend, Evangelist Barbara M. Fountain

thought I was joking. I really thought that I was going to stay home with Aunt Lila and just enjoy my cousins. I actually tried that but Uncle Frank was not having it. He told me a few days after I arrived that they could not support me and I needed to start looking for a job the next day. I came up with several excuses about why I could not find a good job. Uncle Frank had other plans; he bought the paper home for me to look for a job. He drove me to appointments and waited outside for me.

I was hired as a sandwich girl at my first interview. I lasted one day and walked out because I could not take them telling me how to do things or the teasing. I took a bus home and Uncle Frank asked me what happened. I told him that they teased me and I did not like it. He said where is your pay. I told him that I did not have any pay. I did not ask for it. He told me to get in the car because we were going back to get my pay. I told him never mind, it was only one day's pay. He did not care. I got in he car and he told me that I better come out with my pay. I could not believe him, but I did what I was told. He told me to start looking for another job, which I did.

I found a job in a nursing home as a cleaning person. He instructed me how to take two buses to get there, and what time I had to be at the bus stops. I said maybe I should just look for another job because leaving home at 5:00 AM in the morning was too early for me. At that time, I did not understand the lesson he was trying to teach me. I went to work daily and hated that job; it was the worst. I could barely swing the big mop to clean the floors and clean under the beds. The pay was good, but I could not stand the people who were older than me. They teased my because I was the youngest worker there. I kept that job because of the pay. Uncle Frank and Aunt Lila never asked me for any money for rent or food. However, I spent money on my cousins. I loved them and enjoyed spending time with them.

In June of that year, my friend, who had quit school before I did and got married and had a baby, called me. She suggested that I come back to Atlantic City and we could go back to school and go on to college and become nurses. I liked the plan but did not think it could happen. She and several other friends told me that my sister was really acting up and my mother could not control her. I stayed in Richmond a few months longer and decided to go home and try to get back in school. When I returned to Atlantic City, I was in shock at my sister's circumstances; she was pregnant, also. I had to take over the home situation again. My mother had aged and could not handle all that was happening. Her boyfriend was still there. I found a job in the same motel and went to work full time, with my friend still trying to encourage me to return to school. I knew that I could do better than what I was doing.

That February I wrote a letter to the Board of Education and called the principal who was instrumental in expelling me. After several telephone calls, they agreed to meet with me at the Board of Education. I was shocked when I arrived, as there were many people there: School

Superintendent, two principals, a couple of my teachers, truant officer and a juvenile officer. I stated my case, apologized for my previous behaviors and made a promise that I was a changed person and did not hang out with the same people anymore. I had to tell them what I had been doing with myself since I had been expelled and what made me think I could do better this time. I answered every question, they saw that I had truly changed. They told me that they would discuss it and get back to me. They reminded me that if I was allowed to return, I would be 19 years old graduating from high school and they had concerns about that. I told them that I understand but wanted to graduate really bad.

I received a letter from the Board about one month later. The letter asked me to attend another meeting, which I did and was accepted back with many restrictions and demands. I could come back in September. I returned to school at age 18 with a new attitude. I made new friends and was honored and proud to be in school. I worked really hard, kept things in perspective and stayed on track. That previous summer, I met an older guy who I dated. I often took my homework to his apartment on the weekends. I became pregnant that November but knew I could still do it all.

That January I met with the principal and guidance counselor to tell them that I was pregnant but wanted to finish out my Senior year and graduate. The following week, they met with me to inform me that I had proved myself, stayed on the honor roll, and had not missed one

LaVerne Bunn
Senior picture, 1969

day of school   They offered me the Comprehensive Work Study Program, which meant that I attended school in the mornings and worked in the afternoons.   They found me a job at Sears catalogue ordering store on Atlantic Avenue.   I enjoyed this new schedule and pay.   I also became close to a new friend who attended Atlantic City HS with me, a senior as well. (She and I reconnected again recently, after almost 50 years).

My sister had given birth to a baby boy that was the love of my life at that time.   I spent my days with school, caring for my nephew and enjoying my new life.   I prayed that God would give me a baby girl who I would love and give her the best life possible.   I married the man I was dating in

First daughter, Shanyelle

May, graduated in June and God gave me my beautiful baby Girl in August. I was now 19 years old. That summer, I received so many cards from the school, the Board of Ed, the truant officer and the Juvenile Bureau, all congratulating me for my success.

PART SIX

Being a wife, and mother at age 19 was not an easy task, but I enjoyed each and every day of my life and considered this to be another blessing from God. The Lord keeps blessing me.

I was still very active with my family and friends. My friends and I enjoyed our daily routine of taking our babies for walks on the avenue. We all had beautiful and expensive baby carriages. Shanyelle's was a large green Cadillac coach.

I had one sister-in-law at that time and she had a daughter who was a few months older than Shanyelle. We became friends immediately and shared so many wonderful years together and still today we refer to each other as sister-in-law. Our love for each other has always been genuine and strong. Honestly, we were together almost daily with our daughters and I love my niece just as much as I loved her back then. I do miss the fun and laughter that sister in law and I shared. We have secrets that will go to our graves with us.

My second daughter, Sherri-Lyn (Cookie) was born almost three years after Shanyelle's birth. Motherhood to me, was great. My mother often told me that I was an excellent mother and how I took such good care of my

Second daughter,
Sherri-Lyn

children.

We bought a house in Pleasantville, shortly after Cookie was born, and I became active in our new area. I encountered new friends and kept my old friends. I became chairperson of the Pre-school Library Program and was active with Shanyelle's singing on the Rosebud children's choir at church.

We entertained family and friends, and I spent lots of time cooking and baking. I hosted most of the holiday dinners for family. The girls had big birthday parties every year.

My mother remarried to a very nice Christian man, who was a Deacon at our Church. In fact he helped baptize me early on. My mother and I became closer during that time. She was happier and often helped me with my daughters; she was always available to babysit. She was a very good grandmother to my daughters. She loved to babysit them and visited often. She lived 5 minutes away.

As my daughters became older and Shanyelle started

Bridget, Shanyelle and
Sherri-Lyn

school, I wanted more out of myself. I started to take classes at the community college. I got a part time job as a counselor at a juvenile shelter which I was very good at due to my poor behaviors as a juvenile. The director encouraged me to do more. She sent me to several seminars at other colleges and facilities. The director and another staff member, with whom I am still close today, were very instrumental in my growth at that time. I was awarded employee of the year for Atlantic County Juvenile Services. I began to feel very good about myself and my future; however my husband at the time did not appreciate the growth in me. But I did not allow that to stop me. I decided to try something different and applied for a legal secretary position. I was hired on the spot and two weeks later began my new job. A couple of years into my life, things started to go bad in the marriage, and I decided to move out with my daughters and file for a divorce.

I was scared because I had never lived alone, and now I have two children to support. Once we moved, my

Uncle Bubba came to visit the next day to help me get situated.

He brought his daughter, Bridget, who was close to Shanyelle's age and they stayed for one week and I was happy. However when he was getting ready to leave, he told me that he was leaving Bridget with me for the entire summer. So that was the beginning of Bridget being with us often. She spent the summers with us and some holidays.

Bridget, LaVerne and Shanyelle on the Boardwalk

It was during this time that casinos were opening in Atlantic City and my sister worked at one of them. She approached me and suggested that I apply and it paid more than a legal secretary's pay. I told her no because I would not like working at a casino. But my sister insisted that it was best for me to make more money while trying to raise two children. The following week, I applied and was hired immediately as a front desk agent. I was nervous and highly excited for the increase in my finances. It was difficult trying to provide for my daughters and I wanted them to have the best. I was still not comfortable living alone. I was lonely and scared.

Two of my older cousins would visit from Richmond often and my family helped me out as needed.

My manger informed us that he was leaving to open up another casino and wanted five of us to go with him as supervisors. My God, I thought, how are you blessing me so much? Yes, I struggled, but you keep making a way for me and my daughters. I could not believe the blessings. We had started attending another church in Pleasantville but I was not actively involved. My mother had become an Usher and Deaconess and we still visited our home church or, sometimes, she would take my daughters with her.

This new position at this new casino afforded me the ability to better provide for my daughters. However, if their class was going on a trip or having a prom, or any special activity that required more money, I would work overtime, or sometimes work a straight nine days, just to make more money. I did not want my daughters to want or need anything. We did not take vacations but would often go to Richmond for the weekend. Family was and still is very important to me. I still visit my family in Richmond as often as possible.

I was promoted several times at this casino and the last position is when I met my husband and life-long soul-mate.

PART SEVEN

I met Calvin M. Blackwell, Sr. in October 1981. It was a Tuesday evening and I was in the middle of an assignment preparing for a special guest arrival. Calvin had come down from Connecticut on a casino bus rather than drive because he was not feeling good due having a cold. He had been in town for a coupe of days and missed his casino bus to return home. Someone told him to go to the Sands Casino because they would have bus return information for him. He asked someone at the Sands for help and they sent him to me. I told him that I could not find transportation back for him because it was after 8:00 PM and all buses were gone. He explained about the two-day business trip and he needed to get back to Connecticut.

I offered to give him a complimentary room and dinner for the evening and he could return home tomorrow. Calvin asked me to have dinner with him when I got off. I told him that I do NOT fraternize with hotel guests and I am not interested as I needed to get back to my assignment. He reminded me that he is not a guest and did not need anything complimentary because he has his own money. I excused myself and tried to complete my work. He asked me if I could take him home with me when I get off. I said, "Excuse me, did you not hear me?" He was persistent, so I excused myself and walked off to do another task. When I returned, he came back and asked if I could have coffee with him when I got off. I said, "NO. I am going home to my two daughters, because I must return to work tomorrow at 8:00 AM."

Mr. Blackwell would not leave and we began to talk about our children. I learned that we had two children about the same age and we had married and divorced at the same time. We talked a while longer and I had to leave. He asked for my telephone number but I gave him my business card.

LaVerne and Calvin
when they were dating

Well, the next afternoon as I was about to leave my office, the phone rang and when I answered, he said, "Hi, Ms. Hawkins." I knew immediately that it was him. I told him that I was happy that he was able to return home safely but I could not talk to him because I was leaving to get home to my daughters. He asked me to call him later and gave me his telephone number. I had no intentions on calling him but he called me again the next day at work and I told him that I would call him later that evening. Well, I did call him later that evening and I enjoyed talking to him. We began to talk every night. In December, he invited me to come with him on a skiing trip with some friends in Vermont. I thanked him but declined.

We continued our telephone relationship and I began to look forward to his calls and interesting conversations. He invited me to visit in April 1982, and I agreed to visit, but I got sick and could not come. So we continued our daily conversations and he invited to visit him that June. I agreed to visit him at that time. I must say it was a great evening. I took the bus to New York and of course he was late arriving due to traffic and parking. I was about to take a bus back home. We began to page each other over the intercom system but it was constantly busy because we were both paging at the same time. I was deathly afraid of being at the Port Authority and needed to use the lady's room really bad, but was too afraid to go to the lady's room and too afraid to find the bus back to Atlantic City.

I began to swear at myself, and decided to stand beside a pole to make a decision. I looked up and there he was running towards me apologizing as he ran to me. I was so nervous that I began to hit his chest crying that I needed to use the lady's room and I was afraid and where was he and why was he so late. I told him to stand there and do not leave as I was going home. I used the lady's room and felt so much better and decided to stay after his explanation and apology. In his car, Calvin had roses, a bottle of champagne on ice wrapped in a nice white napkin and two champagne glasses. I was truly impressed with my first time in New York City, seeing the lights and buildings. He took me to dinner in a very nice restaurant with a wonderful band playing nice Jazz music. After dinner, we drove to Connecticut. I had never been to Connecticut before either. It was very dark but much different from Pleasantville.

Mother, Mary Corbett and LaVerne in Connecticut

I called my Mother who was caring for my children for the weekend. I spoke to my daughters and decided to enjoy my weekend. Calvin showed me to my room and the guest bathroom and we spent a wonderful evening together. We talked, danced and learned more about each other. He made breakfast the next morning and he took me to dinner that evening. I had to leave Sunday morning, and I knew that I would love and marry this man. I need to mention not only was he a nice man, he was a real looker and dresser.

Our relationship grew and I invited him to visit and meet

my daughters. He told me that he really fell in love with me once her met my girls. Trust me they fell in love with him immediately. I met his children as he kept them during the summer and they went to summer camp while he worked. I was so impressed with him as a single parent as well. He made breakfast, lunch and dinner for his son and daughter each night. He did laundry and was a very good father.

Calvin and LaVerne

We talked of marriage and me and my children moving to Connecticut eventually. Calvin invited me to his sister's birthday party and I met and fell in love with his family. I was excited to meet his family because it was such a large family, and they treated me well. He invited me to his company's holiday party and I met the owner and his wife, and all of his co-workers. I was totally in love with him. My Mother and stepfather really liked Calvin and he was very good to me and my daughters. He made sure that we did not want or need for anything.

My family and friends all loved and enjoyed him. In

February of 1983, I developed a blood clot in my left calf and had to be hospitalized. My mother took my daughters to her home. As soon as I was admitted, I called Calvin to let him know where I was. He was surprised to hear of my condition, but what surprised me was by 9:00 PM that night he walked in to my hospital room. This was through a snow storm. I was shocked but so happy to see him. He told me that he was staying for one week and would pick up my daughters and care for them until he returned home. I called my mother and daughters to let them know that Calvin was here and on the way to pick them up. He was staying for one week and would take care of them. They were so happy. He told me that

Calvin and LaVerne

when he arrived at my mother's house, the girls were on her porch dancing in the snow. He did stay for that week and cared for my children and they visited me everyday. I was absolutely certain without any doubts that this would be my husband. Another blessing from God.

We agreed that I should move to Connecticut that following May and my mother would keep the girls until school ended in June. His children would come at the same time. I missed my children so much, having never been away from them for a month I visited and spent time with them during that month, and was anxious for us to all be a family, the BWell Bunch.

PART EIGHT

I failed to mention that after my discharge from the hospital, Calvin surprised me and bought me a pure bred German Shepherd puppy, which he named Baron. I fell in love with Baron, and when he came to Pleasantville to visit, he always brought Baron. My girls loved Baron as did the neighborhood children, although some were afraid of him. Shanyelle often drove the dog crazy with her blue blanket. I was always afraid that she would hold her blanket up at her bedroom window and tease Baron to get him to jump up and I would yell that the dog was going to jump out of her bedroom window. Cookie was great with Baron, because she listened to Calvin about how to continue to train him, but Shanyelle always had other plans.

We officially became the BWell Bunch in June of 1983. I picked up my children and drove to the airport and picked up our daughter and TC. We drove to Connecticut and all arrived together – how Calvin and I planned it. We did not want either of the children to feel they were there first. Calvin and Baron were waiting for us. Our daughter and TC also fell in love with Baron. I was overexcited about our new family. I had no fear because I knew this was all from God. Calvin and I focused on the children. He wanted me to stay home and be there

-55-

for the children, which I did.

Things were not always easy. Sometimes the children did not get along for various reasons. We realized that blending a family was more difficult than we imaged. We both had similar but different parenting styles. We agreed to combine our parenting styles and things began to work smoother. We paired Shanyelle and our other daughter as a team for chores and TC and Cookie as a team for chores, which worked well for everyone. Everyone had chores, even grocery shopping with me. It actually came down to mostly our daughter shopping with me because she enjoyed our times together and she was more domesticated that the other three. Shanyelle enjoyed being bossy because she was the oldest. TC wanted to be his own boss because he was the only boy and Cookie enjoyed her time playing with Baron or reading. She actually taught Baron to understand her commands in Spanish. This amazed us all.

While Calvin worked, I took the children to the library to checkout books, or to the park. Summer camp was not an option because everyone needed to get to know each other and get along. We decided that we would get married in September because the children had gotten accustomed to our routine and understood that this is our new life. I enrolled the children in school. Shanyelle was a freshman in high school, TC and Cookie were enrolled in the middle school. Our daughter was enrolled in the Sandy Hook Elementary School. We integrated our children into the Newtown school system where there were few other African Americans. After a while, everyone adjusted and began to socialize with their friends. This in itself kept me busy.

We sat with the children and discussed our planned date to get married. We told them that we would have a small wedding with just us and two witnesses because we wanted to stay focused on our family which was very important to us. I shopped for a dress and clothing for the children. Cookie wanted Baron included in the wedding plans but he could not come with us. However, that did not stop her from putting bows on his ears and a pair of her shorts on him.

On September 3, 1983, we all drove to Messiah Baptist Church and were married by Rev Reuben E. Williams, in the presence of our two witnesses. Their son flew in to stand with us. We exchanged wedding bands at that time. A few years later Calvin bought me a diamond. Afterwards we were taken to dinner by our witnesses, a couple we loved so much. In fact as a wedding gift they sent us an upright freezer filled with food.

The children started school and life began for us as a family. Shanyelle did not like high school because she could not identify with the other students, although they were nice to her. She was used to attending a school with her African American friends. One day in early October, she came home from school very upset. It was during a bad rainstorm. I was in bed with a bad cold. She told me that she was running away because she could not take the school anymore. She was crying and truly upset. Nothing I said to her mattered. I told her to please wait and we will call Calvin to come home. She agreed to wait for Calvin to come home and they went to the diner and talked until 9:00 PM. It was like whatever he said to her changed her mind and her mind set. She became a new person and took control, never mentioned running away again.

We made a rule in our home that anyone could call a family meeting at anytime. It appeared that we were having family meetings every week because of true sibling issues. They enjoyed putting on talent shows for us and we played games. Shanyelle joined the basketball team and took up sewing. TC played football and sung on the school choir. Cookie joined the band and cheer-leaders. Our other daughter joined the school choir and enjoyed her homemaking class.

My mother and stepfather came to visit often as did my family from Richmond. The girls visited my mother for weeks in the summer and TC visited his grandmother in Bridgeport for a couple of weeks. TC had more friends that lived close by so he was content to stay home. Our niece and nephew often spent weekends with us during the summer. We always seemed to have a house full. We entertained our families often – we were busy. I took a part time job and started taking a few classes at the community college. Calvin left his company to open his own business.

LaVerne and Calvin
leaving church services

We joined Messiah Baptist Church and became very busy, me as an Usher and Calvin as a Trustee. I was soon ordained a Deaconess, which made me so proud as I knew that my calling was to be a servant. The girls got baptized and got busy as well. I need to mention that Thanksgiving and Christmas were our best holidays. I loved cooking and we all enjoyed entertaining and having company since we lived so far out from everyone. Christmas in our house was always a great time. Calvin would write notes for each child with hints to where their gifts could be found. They loved it and he enjoyed buying big gifts for them. They had big Christmases. Calvin and I often took time for ourselves as far as going out to dinner.

We finally took our first vacation away from the children when Shanyelle was a senior in high school. My mother came up to stay with the children. She was hard of hearing and I understand that they took advantage of that. We laughed later on when they finally told us of the crazy things they did when we were away for that week.

Life was good, but the children were older and always wanted or needed the most expensive things. We tried to give them just about everything that wanted.

Calvin was strict about the dating situation especially with Shanyelle because she was our first to start dating. The one story that we still laugh at is he told her to be home by 11:00 PM. She called about 10:30 and asked to stay out a little longer because they were going to McDonald's. He told her to bring him a milkshake home. She was so upset with him. She knew that he really did not want that milkshake. In fact, she had to wake him up to hand the milkshake to him. Before we knew it, there were proms and pre-prom parties and it was time for Shanyelle to go to college. She was accepted at UCONN and she was happy. I could not believe that time flew by so fast. Our first was getting ready for college.

PART NINE

Shanyelle attended the CAP Program for the summer prior to starting that August. She met many friends during that time. Most are still very close today. We often laugh at our attendance at Family Day. She asked me to prepare so much food and we all were excited to see her. Once we arrived, she greeted us and introduced us to her friends and we barely saw her the remainder of the afternoon. Driving home, we all were so angry with her, since she did not eat lunch with us or join us for anything. However, we noted that the other parents were siting alone as well. We did not care. We came to visit as her family, her brother, her sisters and her parents.

By this time there was no *mine* or *yours*, everything was *ours* – our parents, our siblings, etc. I must say her siblings were quite upset with her that day. I was just as upset. Calvin understood more so than any of us. I also want to note that Calvin and Shanyelle have always had their own relationship. When they argued among themselves, we all stayed out of it. They have loud voices and we never knew what was going on. Today their relationship remains the same. When the two of them are in a heated discussion, we still stay away. Her husband and children do the same. They are both Virgos.

When Shanyelle went away to college, I became ill and did not know what was wrong with me. I had headaches, stiff neck, stomach issues and was seen by many doctors. I had several medical tests but they could not find anything wrong with me. My doctor finally told me that all of my tests were negative. He told me that I was just stressed because our daughter left home for college. Once that was established, I was fine. College was good for Shanyelle. She enjoyed it and grew. However, she had to take a class during the summer, and we told her and the other three, if they messed up at anytime, they would have to pay for summer classes. She worked and paid for that class and never had to take another summer class.

That following year, we had to prepare for TC to go to college. He did not know where he wanted to go to college. He only knew that he wanted to play football at college. He finally decided to attend Ulster and he did play football for a while. We had two children in college and two other on the way. Again, but God, where was the money coming from? I was still working part time. God has blessed us more than we could ever think of. Again I got sick with the same issues and my doctor reminded me of what I had just experienced the year before. I really missed our two older children. The house was quiet with just Cookie and our other daughter home.

At holidays and breaks we had everyone home again. I was happy but glad when they returned to school because now we had the four children and they both brought friends home or went out and friends spent the night, and Shanyelle always said I was strict with her friends as well.

Daughter, Sherri-Lyn (Cookie)

The next year it was time for Cookie to go to college and she started at University of New Haven and transferred to Southern Connecticut University where she obtained a double major and continued to excel in Spanish as she studied Spanish from Middle School throughout college. College was different for Cookie. Each semester she had to be convinced to return. She had a wonderful GPA but always threatened to drop out of college. She was very bright and intelligent, fluent in Spanish, and was my Spanish tutor when I attended college. With three children in college, our home became very quiet. Our other daughter always said I love my siblings but it gets crazy when they are home.

Shanyelle became a mentor in her junior year. She mentored four young boys from one of the projects in Hartford and yes, you guessed it, they came home with her some weekends. And she always hit dad up for money because the boys needed sneakers or something. We enjoyed having them, they were funny and appreciative of anything we did for them. We are still in contact with two of them today. They always called us Mr. and Mrs. Black.

During the busyness with our family, we continued to be active in church and joined several ministries. We also became very close to several other couples in church and started to travel together at least twice per year. We often had dinners and breakfasts together throughout the year.

In addition to vacationing with our church friends, we have also vacationed with Calvin's family. Our favorite was spending time in Georgia for several days at his cousin's home.

I met one of Calvin's choir members and we became close. She was very instrumental in me becoming an employee for the State of Connecticut. I started a full time position as a social service assistant for the Department of Children and Families, a position that I loved and truly enjoyed – my servant gift from God. It was while working in this field, that I decided to return to college full time to obtain my degree. However, I was still serving as an Usher and was asked to become a Deaconess at Messiah Baptist. I had to pray earnestly for God's help to get me through a full time job, a full time student at Albertus Magnus College and walking as a Deaconess. My husband helped me so much with our home and with my homework. I know that I could not have made it without his support and God's favor over my life.

It was finally time for our other daughter to go to college, and of course I became ill again. She started at Waterbury Community College and then transferred to Southern Connecticut University. Now our home was so quiet but I was not home to enjoy the peace and quiet because I was so busy. I went to school on weekends, and evenings and if I had the opportunity to take an extra credit, I would fit it in. It took me a total of two years to complete my degree.

We were all home for the holidays and life fell in place and we were a family again. One year our nephew asked if he could stay with us until he completed his final year at Southern Connecticut University. We agreed that he could stay but had to follow the rules of the house, although he was a couple of years older. He complied.

It was also at the time that my stepfather passed and my mother came to live with us. "Don't know how we did it, but we did." God has been our anchor forever. I still thank God for all that he has done for us and continues to do. I thank God for my husband who took care of our daughters as if they were his biological children. None of the children ever wanted for anything. Calvin worked hard at his business and he was good at what he did. He has a design and build business and has always been sought after because of his eye and gift of design.

In 1996, I graduated from Albertus Magnus College with a 3.4 GPA. My husband and children threw me a surprise graduation party that I will never forget. There were at least two hundred or more people, right in our home. It was catered, had a DJ, and friends and family were there. There was a dance floor and we had a great time. I was also promoted to a social worker, after taking and passing the exam. But God.

My aunt Lila and uncle Frank along with everyone else attended my graduation and surprise party. My aunt Lila had been diagnosed with cancer but she was here for me.

Shanyelle and Brent,
daughter and son-in-law

Shanyelle met Brent Young right out of college and we loved him. He is still the best son-in-law that we have. They got married in August, 1993 and gave us the best gift as grandparents. They had twins, Brent, Jr. and Shaylyn, in October, 1994. Of course, I took a leave of absence from my job and stayed there for six weeks. I did come home maybe twice a week and continued attending college as well. We were such proud grandparents. Calvin could not contain himself at

LaVerne and Calvin at Shanyelle and Brent's wedding

the birth of the twins. We were waiting with the paternal grandparents, when Brent came out to tell us that Shanyelle was about to give birth, Calvin ran in with Brent, leaving us in shock. He saw the babies before we did. We were so happy and proud. We agreed to keep the twins one weekend every month from Friday until Sunday evening to give them a break. We kept our word until they were maybe thirteen years old. We also sent them to summer camp each summer for one week,

In July, 1996, I was ordained as a Deaconess by Rev. Reuben E. Williams, another proud time in my life. I was so emotionally overwhelmed that I could not speak. My husband had to come down from the choir loft to hold me up. Subsequently our church ordained all female Deaconess to Deacons. Therefore, I am now Deacon LaVerne Blackwell.

In October 1996, our son, Calvin M. Blackwell, Jr. (TC), got sick and passed away. This was a very difficult time in our lives. His siblings could not understand this and it was hard to move on afterwards. He was 26 years old

– too young to loose him. We know that God knew best. We will always remember him and still speak of the good and fun times we had with him for the period God allowed us to have him.

In November 1996, I transferred to the Danbury office and became the only high risk newborn specialist that office ever hired.

On August 1, 1997 my beautiful Aunt Lila Archer passed. She was a woman like no other. She was my mentor and friend. She was the family matriarch and gave her all to us. She loved us unconditionally.

PART TEN

I enjoyed being the high risk newborn specialist. It was a busy and stressful position. I basically had all of the newborn cases in our office. I loved visiting the babies and ensuring their safety.

On August 1, 1997 my wonderful aunt and friend Lila passed away. What a devastation and loss to our family. She was truly our family matriarch, and her death was a major void to our family.

During my time at the Danbury office, I developed many close friendships, but the main friendship was with the Sistah Girls. There were six of us, and our group started off as a Bible study on Tuesday evenings. The Bible studies lead to several of us taking classes at a church to be certified as evangelist and counselors. We completed the two-year classes and graduated and became certified. This friendship lasted for many years and continues to-day. We have traveled together in and out of the country.

My stepfather passed and my mother came to live with us for a couple of years and returned to Atlantic City where she passed on May 31, 1999.

Also during my career at the Danbury office, I was promoted to supervisor of treatment services and also as supervisor of investigations unit, positions that I enjoyed. I retired from the Danbury office as an administrative case review supervisor.

Our life continued to be busy. Calvin surprised me one Christmas with a 3-caret diamond ring. Truly it was a Christmas that I will never forget. As usual, his surprises were always labeled with a note that said, "find me." I searched all over for this surprise. I looked in the freezer, under the couches and could not find my gift. He had it hidden in the middle of the Christmas tree, wrapped in a beautiful gift box inside of two gift boxes.

Although life gets busy there are incidents and issues that can rock your world so hard that you think you cannot make it through. But with faith you somehow make it. One of those times for me was losing my cousin, Joan, on September 15, 2014. Joan was a big part of my life. She was the first born of my Uncle Frank and Aunt Lila. We grew up together as sisters and best friends. We had many very good times and laughter together. I will always love and remember her.

On August 5, 2018, I lost my one and only sister, Francine. Again, through my faith and God, I made it through. I sometimes feel lost without her because as she always said, "We are all that we have." There were times that we did not see eye to eye, but we always found a way to overcome whatever issues we had. Now that

Uncles, Frank standing and Joe sitting, with sister Francine and LaVerne

Sister, Francine

she is no longer with me in person, I know she is with me in spirit, and we continue to have our relationship.

Last year, February of 2019, I decided at the last minute that I would throw myself a birthday party because I have never had a party in all of my years. I always celebrate my birthday in someway, mostly for the entire month, but this time I wanted to celebrate it BIG. It was a last minute decision but with the help of my two friends, Terri and Annie, we moved it right along. However, I need to say that our daughter, Shanyelle stepped in and ran away with it. Between Shanyelle and Calvin, they managed to surprise me by having my best friend from 5th grade, Barbara, come as my surprise. I must say it was a wonderful time and I enjoyed it to the fullest. Shanyelle said she has never seen me so happy in all of her life. I thank everyone who attended and made my day special.

I decided to write this book about my life because I always wanted it to be known that God has always been there for me. He has carried me through and blessed me in so many ways. Often, when I share a piece of my life, people are often shocked and do not believe that I made it this far. Even Barbara, as close as we are, did not know all that I had been through, but we both know that God can do miracles.

God has done and continues to do miracles and blessings in this family. Our daughters are successful with their careers and have done extremely well. We are also very proud of our wonderful grandchildren. Our twin grandson is a doctor – the first doctor in our family. Our granddaughter is a therapist – her concentration is in autism. She is also a successful author. Their younger brother is completing his last year of college as a finance major.

This is the first year since the twins were babies that we did not go on our yearly family vacation. We usually rent a large house and enjoy the entire week together as a family. Often our family from Richmond joins us.

As I write this book, we are still in a pandemic, COVID-19. Many lives have been lost and it is a very sad time for many people. But again, I have to thank my God everyday for seeing us through and being a fence around us. Churches are closed, stores and restaurants are closed, we are wearing masks and gloves to go outside of our homes. People cannot have proper burials. I have never seen anything like this in my life. We are all staying in out homes. It was during a conversation with Shanyelle during this pandemic, she suggested that this is a good time for me to write my story and possibly help me get out of some of my past pain. I took her up on that suggestion and have cried during much of this writing. I thank her for her encouragement to take this project on, but I also need to thank my husband, Calvin M. Blackwell, because he has helped me get this project completed.

I will mention that during this pandemic, my Aunt Victoria, who also took care of me as a child in Amelia, passed and it hurt so bad that I could not go to say goodbye to her.

I want to mention that I also lost one of my loving sister-in-laws during this pandemic. Thankfully we were able to have a beautiful internment for her.

Writing this memoir has given me some healing. I cried often while writing about my pain. I know there are many LaVernes in this world and pray that they too could receive healing as I have. I will end this book by thanking God for my Truths, my Triumphs, and my GOD.

Niece Bridget Harris

LaVerne and Calvin
as newlyweds

Granny with her
grandchildren, Brent, Jr.,
Shaylyn and Shan at
Martha Vineyards

Shanyelle and
Sherri-Lyn singing
"She's a Special Lady"
to their mother, LaVerne